My Home Inventory Organizer

This organizer belongs to:

Name:

Phone number:

E-mail:

Insurance Company:

Insurance Contact Phone number:

Insurance Policy Number:

My Home Inventory Organizer

First Edition

Arlington Books and Software

www.arlington.com.au

Also by Robert J. Pemberton

My Website Password Organizer
My To Do List
My Address Book
My Goals
My Ideas
My Vehicle Log Book
My Music Collection
My Movie Collection
My Favorite Recipes
My Book of Lists
My Home Maintenance Records
My Income/Expense Records
My Friendship Book
My Baby Book
My Scrap Book

View the full book list at:
www.arlington.com.au

Insurance Tip

Store your inventory organizer in a secure location outside of your home or in a fire proof safe.

For more tips, visit www.arlington.com.au

ITEM NAME:
Description:

Location/Room:
Make:
Model:
Serial Number:
Color:
Warranty/Guarantee Period:
Purchased From:
Supplier Address:
Supplier Contact Number:
Purchase Date:
Purchase Price:
Receipt/Ref Number:
Current Value:
Quantity:
Condition:
Notes:

Staple or paste the item Receipt and/or Photo here.

ITEM NAME:

Description:

Location/Room:

Make:

Model:

Serial Number:

Color:

Warranty/Guarantee Period:

Purchased From:

Supplier Address:

Supplier Contact Number:

Purchase Date:

Purchase Price:

Receipt/Ref Number:

Current Value:

Quantity:

Condition:

Notes:

Staple or paste the item Receipt and/or Photo here.

ITEM NAME:
Description:

Location/Room:
Make:
Model:
Serial Number:
Color:
Warranty/Guarantee Period:
Purchased From:
Supplier Address:
Supplier Contact Number:
Purchase Date:
Purchase Price:
Receipt/Ref Number:
Current Value:
Quantity:
Condition:
Notes:

Staple or paste the item Receipt and/or Photo here.

ITEM NAME:

Description:

Location/Room:

Make:

Model:

Serial Number:

Color:

Warranty/Guarantee Period:

Purchased From:

Supplier Address:

Supplier Contact Number:

Purchase Date:

Purchase Price:

Receipt/Ref Number:

Current Value:

Quantity:

Condition:

Notes:

Staple or paste the item Receipt and/or Photo here.

ITEM NAME:

Description:

Location/Room:

Make:

Model:

Serial Number:

Color:

Warranty/Guarantee Period:

Purchased From:

Supplier Address:

Supplier Contact Number:

Purchase Date:

Purchase Price:

Receipt/Ref Number:

Current Value:

Quantity:

Condition:

Notes:

Staple or paste the item Receipt and/or Photo here.

ITEM NAME:
Description:

Location/Room:
Make:
Model:
Serial Number:
Color:
Warranty/Guarantee Period:
Purchased From:
Supplier Address:
Supplier Contact Number:
Purchase Date:
Purchase Price:
Receipt/Ref Number:
Current Value:
Quantity:
Condition:
Notes:

Staple or paste the item Receipt and/or Photo here.

ITEM NAME:
Description:

Location/Room:
Make:
Model:
Serial Number:
Color:
Warranty/Guarantee Period:
Purchased From:
Supplier Address:
Supplier Contact Number:
Purchase Date:
Purchase Price:
Receipt/Ref Number:
Current Value:
Quantity:
Condition:
Notes:

Staple or paste the item Receipt and/or Photo here.

ITEM NAME:

Description:

Location/Room:

Make:

Model:

Serial Number:

Color:

Warranty/Guarantee Period:

Purchased From:

Supplier Address:

Supplier Contact Number:

Purchase Date:

Purchase Price:

Receipt/Ref Number:

Current Value:

Quantity:

Condition:

Notes:

Staple or paste the item Receipt and/or Photo here.

ITEM NAME:
Description:

Location/Room:
Make:
Model:
Serial Number:
Color:
Warranty/Guarantee Period:
Purchased From:
Supplier Address:
Supplier Contact Number:
Purchase Date:
Purchase Price:
Receipt/Ref Number:
Current Value:
Quantity:
Condition:
Notes:

Staple or paste the item Receipt and/or Photo here.

ITEM NAME:
Description:

Location/Room:
Make:
Model:
Serial Number:
Color:
Warranty/Guarantee Period:
Purchased From:
Supplier Address:
Supplier Contact Number:
Purchase Date:
Purchase Price:
Receipt/Ref Number:
Current Value:
Quantity:
Condition:
Notes:

Staple or paste the item Receipt and/or Photo here.

ITEM NAME:
Description:

Location/Room:
Make:
Model:
Serial Number:
Color:
Warranty/Guarantee Period:
Purchased From:
Supplier Address:
Supplier Contact Number:
Purchase Date:
Purchase Price:
Receipt/Ref Number:
Current Value:
Quantity:
Condition:
Notes:

Staple or paste the item Receipt and/or Photo here.

ITEM NAME:
Description:

Location/Room:
Make:
Model:
Serial Number:
Color:
Warranty/Guarantee Period:
Purchased From:
Supplier Address:
Supplier Contact Number:
Purchase Date:
Purchase Price:
Receipt/Ref Number:
Current Value:
Quantity:
Condition:
Notes:

Staple or paste the item Receipt and/or Photo here.

ITEM NAME:
Description:

Location/Room:
Make:
Model:
Serial Number:
Color:
Warranty/Guarantee Period:
Purchased From:
Supplier Address:
Supplier Contact Number:
Purchase Date:
Purchase Price:
Receipt/Ref Number:
Current Value:
Quantity:
Condition:
Notes:

Staple or paste the item Receipt and/or Photo here.

ITEM NAME:
Description:

Location/Room:
Make:
Model:
Serial Number:
Color:
Warranty/Guarantee Period:
Purchased From:
Supplier Address:
Supplier Contact Number:
Purchase Date:
Purchase Price:
Receipt/Ref Number:
Current Value:
Quantity:
Condition:
Notes:

Staple or paste the item Receipt and/or Photo here.

ITEM NAME:

Description:

Location/Room:

Make:

Model:

Serial Number:

Color:

Warranty/Guarantee Period:

Purchased From:

Supplier Address:

Supplier Contact Number:

Purchase Date:

Purchase Price:

Receipt/Ref Number:

Current Value:

Quantity:

Condition:

Notes:

Staple or paste the item Receipt and/or Photo here.

ITEM NAME:
Description:

Location/Room:
Make:
Model:
Serial Number:
Color:
Warranty/Guarantee Period:
Purchased From:
Supplier Address:
Supplier Contact Number:
Purchase Date:
Purchase Price:
Receipt/Ref Number:
Current Value:
Quantity:
Condition:
Notes:

Staple or paste the item Receipt and/or Photo here.

ITEM NAME:

Description:

Location/Room:

Make:

Model:

Serial Number:

Color:

Warranty/Guarantee Period:

Purchased From:

Supplier Address:

Supplier Contact Number:

Purchase Date:

Purchase Price:

Receipt/Ref Number:

Current Value:

Quantity:

Condition:

Notes:

Staple or paste the item Receipt and/or Photo here.

ITEM NAME:
Description:

Location/Room:
Make:
Model:
Serial Number:
Color:
Warranty/Guarantee Period:
Purchased From:
Supplier Address:
Supplier Contact Number:
Purchase Date:
Purchase Price:
Receipt/Ref Number:
Current Value:
Quantity:
Condition:
Notes:

Staple or paste the item Receipt and/or Photo here.

ITEM NAME:
Description:

Location/Room:
Make:
Model:
Serial Number:
Color:
Warranty/Guarantee Period:
Purchased From:
Supplier Address:
Supplier Contact Number:
Purchase Date:
Purchase Price:
Receipt/Ref Number:
Current Value:
Quantity:
Condition:
Notes:

Staple or paste the item Receipt and/or Photo here.

ITEM NAME:

Description:

Location/Room:

Make:

Model:

Serial Number:

Color:

Warranty/Guarantee Period:

Purchased From:

Supplier Address:

Supplier Contact Number:

Purchase Date:

Purchase Price:

Receipt/Ref Number:

Current Value:

Quantity:

Condition:

Notes:

Staple or paste the item Receipt and/or Photo here.

ITEM NAME:
Description:

Location/Room:
Make:
Model:
Serial Number:
Color:
Warranty/Guarantee Period:
Purchased From:
Supplier Address:
Supplier Contact Number:
Purchase Date:
Purchase Price:
Receipt/Ref Number:
Current Value:
Quantity:
Condition:
Notes:

Staple or paste the item Receipt and/or Photo here.

ITEM NAME:

Description:

Location/Room:

Make:

Model:

Serial Number:

Color:

Warranty/Guarantee Period:

Purchased From:

Supplier Address:

Supplier Contact Number:

Purchase Date:

Purchase Price:

Receipt/Ref Number:

Current Value:

Quantity:

Condition:

Notes:

Staple or paste the item Receipt and/or Photo here.

ITEM NAME:

Description:

Location/Room:

Make:

Model:

Serial Number:

Color:

Warranty/Guarantee Period:

Purchased From:

Supplier Address:

Supplier Contact Number:

Purchase Date:

Purchase Price:

Receipt/Ref Number:

Current Value:

Quantity:

Condition:

Notes:

Staple or paste the item Receipt and/or Photo here.

ITEM NAME:

Description:

Location/Room:

Make:

Model:

Serial Number:

Color:

Warranty/Guarantee Period:

Purchased From:

Supplier Address:

Supplier Contact Number:

Purchase Date:

Purchase Price:

Receipt/Ref Number:

Current Value:

Quantity:

Condition:

Notes:

Staple or paste the item Receipt and/or Photo here.

ITEM NAME:

Description:

Location/Room:

Make:

Model:

Serial Number:

Color:

Warranty/Guarantee Period:

Purchased From:

Supplier Address:

Supplier Contact Number:

Purchase Date:

Purchase Price:

Receipt/Ref Number:

Current Value:

Quantity:

Condition:

Notes:

Staple or paste the item Receipt and/or Photo here.

ITEM NAME:
Description:

Location/Room:
Make:
Model:
Serial Number:
Color:
Warranty/Guarantee Period:
Purchased From:
Supplier Address:
Supplier Contact Number:
Purchase Date:
Purchase Price:
Receipt/Ref Number:
Current Value:
Quantity:
Condition:
Notes:

Staple or paste the item Receipt and/or Photo here.

ITEM NAME:
Description:

Location/Room:
Make:
Model:
Serial Number:
Color:
Warranty/Guarantee Period:
Purchased From:
Supplier Address:
Supplier Contact Number:
Purchase Date:
Purchase Price:
Receipt/Ref Number:
Current Value:
Quantity:
Condition:
Notes:

Staple or paste the item Receipt and/or Photo here.

ITEM NAME:
Description:

Location/Room:
Make:
Model:
Serial Number:
Color:
Warranty/Guarantee Period:
Purchased From:
Supplier Address:
Supplier Contact Number:
Purchase Date:
Purchase Price:
Receipt/Ref Number:
Current Value:
Quantity:
Condition:
Notes:

Staple or paste the item Receipt and/or Photo here.

ITEM NAME:

Description:

Location/Room:

Make:

Model:

Serial Number:

Color:

Warranty/Guarantee Period:

Purchased From:

Supplier Address:

Supplier Contact Number:

Purchase Date:

Purchase Price:

Receipt/Ref Number:

Current Value:

Quantity:

Condition:

Notes:

Staple or paste the item Receipt and/or Photo here.

ITEM NAME:

Description:

Location/Room:

Make:

Model:

Serial Number:

Color:

Warranty/Guarantee Period:

Purchased From:

Supplier Address:

Supplier Contact Number:

Purchase Date:

Purchase Price:

Receipt/Ref Number:

Current Value:

Quantity:

Condition:

Notes:

Staple or paste the item Receipt and/or Photo here.

ITEM NAME:

Description:

Location/Room:

Make:

Model:

Serial Number:

Color:

Warranty/Guarantee Period:

Purchased From:

Supplier Address:

Supplier Contact Number:

Purchase Date:

Purchase Price:

Receipt/Ref Number:

Current Value:

Quantity:

Condition:

Notes:

Staple or paste the item Receipt and/or Photo here.

ITEM NAME:

Description:

Location/Room:

Make:

Model:

Serial Number:

Color:

Warranty/Guarantee Period:

Purchased From:

Supplier Address:

Supplier Contact Number:

Purchase Date:

Purchase Price:

Receipt/Ref Number:

Current Value:

Quantity:

Condition:

Notes:

Staple or paste the item Receipt and/or Photo here.

ITEM NAME:

Description:

Location/Room:

Make:

Model:

Serial Number:

Color:

Warranty/Guarantee Period:

Purchased From:

Supplier Address:

Supplier Contact Number:

Purchase Date:

Purchase Price:

Receipt/Ref Number:

Current Value:

Quantity:

Condition:

Notes:

Staple or paste the item Receipt and/or Photo here.

ITEM NAME:
Description:

Location/Room:
Make:
Model:
Serial Number:
Color:
Warranty/Guarantee Period:
Purchased From:
Supplier Address:
Supplier Contact Number:
Purchase Date:
Purchase Price:
Receipt/Ref Number:
Current Value:
Quantity:
Condition:
Notes:

Staple or paste the item Receipt and/or Photo here.

ITEM NAME:
Description:

Location/Room:
Make:
Model:
Serial Number:
Color:
Warranty/Guarantee Period:
Purchased From:
Supplier Address:
Supplier Contact Number:
Purchase Date:
Purchase Price:
Receipt/Ref Number:
Current Value:
Quantity:
Condition:
Notes:

Staple or paste the item Receipt and/or Photo here.

ITEM NAME:

Description:

Location/Room:

Make:

Model:

Serial Number:

Color:

Warranty/Guarantee Period:

Purchased From:

Supplier Address:

Supplier Contact Number:

Purchase Date:

Purchase Price:

Receipt/Ref Number:

Current Value:

Quantity:

Condition:

Notes:

Staple or paste the item Receipt and/or Photo here.

ITEM NAME:
Description:

Location/Room:
Make:
Model:
Serial Number:
Color:
Warranty/Guarantee Period:
Purchased From:
Supplier Address:
Supplier Contact Number:
Purchase Date:
Purchase Price:
Receipt/Ref Number:
Current Value:
Quantity:
Condition:
Notes:

Staple or paste the item Receipt and/or Photo here.

ITEM NAME:

Description:

Location/Room:

Make:

Model:

Serial Number:

Color:

Warranty/Guarantee Period:

Purchased From:

Supplier Address:

Supplier Contact Number:

Purchase Date:

Purchase Price:

Receipt/Ref Number:

Current Value:

Quantity:

Condition:

Notes:

Staple or paste the item Receipt and/or Photo here.

ITEM NAME:

Description:

Location/Room:

Make:

Model:

Serial Number:

Color:

Warranty/Guarantee Period:

Purchased From:

Supplier Address:

Supplier Contact Number:

Purchase Date:

Purchase Price:

Receipt/Ref Number:

Current Value:

Quantity:

Condition:

Notes:

Staple or paste the item Receipt and/or Photo here.

ITEM NAME:

Description:

Location/Room:

Make:

Model:

Serial Number:

Color:

Warranty/Guarantee Period:

Purchased From:

Supplier Address:

Supplier Contact Number:

Purchase Date:

Purchase Price:

Receipt/Ref Number:

Current Value:

Quantity:

Condition:

Notes:

Staple or paste the item Receipt and/or Photo here.

ITEM NAME:

Description:

Location/Room:

Make:

Model:

Serial Number:

Color:

Warranty/Guarantee Period:

Purchased From:

Supplier Address:

Supplier Contact Number:

Purchase Date:

Purchase Price:

Receipt/Ref Number:

Current Value:

Quantity:

Condition:

Notes:

Staple or paste the item Receipt and/or Photo here.

ITEM NAME:

Description:

Location/Room:

Make:

Model:

Serial Number:

Color:

Warranty/Guarantee Period:

Purchased From:

Supplier Address:

Supplier Contact Number:

Purchase Date:

Purchase Price:

Receipt/Ref Number:

Current Value:

Quantity:

Condition:

Notes:

Staple or paste the item Receipt and/or Photo here.

ITEM NAME:
Description:

Location/Room:
Make:
Model:
Serial Number:
Color:
Warranty/Guarantee Period:
Purchased From:
Supplier Address:
Supplier Contact Number:
Purchase Date:
Purchase Price:
Receipt/Ref Number:
Current Value:
Quantity:
Condition:
Notes:

Staple or paste the item Receipt and/or Photo here.

ITEM NAME:
Description:

Location/Room:
Make:
Model:
Serial Number:
Color:
Warranty/Guarantee Period:
Purchased From:
Supplier Address:
Supplier Contact Number:
Purchase Date:
Purchase Price:
Receipt/Ref Number:
Current Value:
Quantity:
Condition:
Notes:

Staple or paste the item Receipt and/or Photo here.

ITEM NAME:
Description:

Location/Room:
Make:
Model:
Serial Number:
Color:
Warranty/Guarantee Period:
Purchased From:
Supplier Address:
Supplier Contact Number:
Purchase Date:
Purchase Price:
Receipt/Ref Number:
Current Value:
Quantity:
Condition:
Notes:

Staple or paste the item Receipt and/or Photo here.

ITEM NAME:

Description:

Location/Room:

Make:

Model:

Serial Number:

Color:

Warranty/Guarantee Period:

Purchased From:

Supplier Address:

Supplier Contact Number:

Purchase Date:

Purchase Price:

Receipt/Ref Number:

Current Value:

Quantity:

Condition:

Notes:

Staple or paste the item Receipt and/or Photo here.

ITEM NAME:
Description:

Location/Room:
Make:
Model:
Serial Number:
Color:
Warranty/Guarantee Period:
Purchased From:
Supplier Address:
Supplier Contact Number:
Purchase Date:
Purchase Price:
Receipt/Ref Number:
Current Value:
Quantity:
Condition:
Notes:

Staple or paste the item Receipt and/or Photo here.

ITEM NAME:
Description:

Location/Room:
Make:
Model:
Serial Number:
Color:
Warranty/Guarantee Period:
Purchased From:
Supplier Address:
Supplier Contact Number:
Purchase Date:
Purchase Price:
Receipt/Ref Number:
Current Value:
Quantity:
Condition:
Notes:

Staple or paste the item Receipt and/or Photo here.

ITEM NAME:
Description:

Location/Room:
Make:
Model:
Serial Number:
Color:
Warranty/Guarantee Period:
Purchased From:
Supplier Address:
Supplier Contact Number:
Purchase Date:
Purchase Price:
Receipt/Ref Number:
Current Value:
Quantity:
Condition:
Notes:

Staple or paste the item Receipt and/or Photo here.

ITEM NAME:

Description:

Location/Room:

Make:

Model:

Serial Number:

Color:

Warranty/Guarantee Period:

Purchased From:

Supplier Address:

Supplier Contact Number:

Purchase Date:

Purchase Price:

Receipt/Ref Number:

Current Value:

Quantity:

Condition:

Notes:

Staple or paste the item Receipt and/or Photo here.

ITEM NAME:
Description:

Location/Room:
Make:
Model:
Serial Number:
Color:
Warranty/Guarantee Period:
Purchased From:
Supplier Address:
Supplier Contact Number:
Purchase Date:
Purchase Price:
Receipt/Ref Number:
Current Value:
Quantity:
Condition:
Notes:

Staple or paste the item Receipt and/or Photo here.

Notes:

NOTES

Notes:

NOTES

Notes:

NOTES

CPSIA information can be obtained at www.ICGtesting.com
Printed in the USA
LVOW01s1719310813

350427LV00023B/654/P